Plantains in the Rain
selected Chinese poems of Du Mu

Du Mu (AD 803–852) was born into an aristocratic family which became impoverished during his lifetime in the latter part of the Tang dynasty. His work belongs to last period of classical Chinese poetry's golden age and he is traditionally paired together with China's most famous poet, Du Fu, as the respected lesser half of 'Big and Little Du'. Du Mu is particularly well known for his superb quatrains.

Richard F Burton is a senior lecturer in physiology at the University of Glasgow. Most of his writings are scientific, but he has published essays, poems and translations in a number of magazines. His interest in literary Chinese dates from his early childhood when he was first given a book on the subject. Dr Burton is also a jazz musician in his spare time.

Wellsweep Chinese Poets 3

Du Mu

Plantains
in the Rain

selected
Chinese poems
of Du Mu
translated by
R F Burton

wellsweep

ACKNOWLEDGEMENTS

The calligraphy on the title page and front cover and
accompanying nine of the poems in this book is by Mr Joseph Lo.
The cover illustration is reproduced from a famous piece of
calligraphy in Du Mu's own handwriting, the *Zhang Haohao shi*.

First published in 1990 by
Wellsweep Press
719 Fulham Road
London SW6 5UL

0 948454 08 3 trade edition (laminated cover)
0 948454 58 X readers' edition (laid paper cover)

The publisher gratefully acknowledges the financial assistance of
the Arts Council of Great Britain.

Designed and set by Wellsweep
Printed by E & E Plumridge, Linton, Cambridge

For Lin Po,

in gratitude for
her help
and encouragement

CONTENTS

Please note:
An asterisk beside the title of a poems indicates that
there is a note in this section of the book.

INTRODUCTION

More than forty eight thousand poems survive from the Tang dynasty (618–907 AD). Through these we may remind ourselves of the constancy of human nature and delight in glimpses of a culture far distant in time and space. The Chinese still read these old poems, though they generally now give the characters their modern pronunciations. Du Mu (also spelled Tu Mu in the earlier romanization) wrote thousands of poems, but burnt all but a dozen of those in his possession. We are fortunate that about five hundred survive, thanks mainly to the work of one of Du Mu's nephews. Most of these, and nearly all in this collection, are of four or eight lines. Du Mu is best known for his deft quatrains. Some authors remark on the general cheerfulness of his poems while others note their pessimism.

For the most part, I have selected poems that require little background knowledge or annotation for their appreciation, but since these are helpful I give here a short account of Du Mu's life. Translating from Chinese to English is very different from translating between related European languages and therefore I shall also say something about the form of the original poems and about my own approach to their translation.

DU MU — THE MAN

Du Mu was born in 803 near the capital city of Chang'an (near present-day Xi'an) into an aristocratic family. He was the grandson of a prime minister and started his life surrounded by wealth and culture. However, the family fortune quickly dwindled after his grandfather died in 812. As his father passed on only a few years later, Du Mu was unable to embark on a study of the classics — so necessary to a political career in those days — until he was twenty. Even with this late start he managed to pass the civil service examination when only twenty five, obtaining the prestigious, highest degree of *jinshi*. In spite of this early success, his talents received far less recognition than he had hoped. His lack of promotion at court was partly due to his honest and upright nature and to his unwillingness to toady to the powerful. It did not help that he spent time caring for a younger brother who was going blind.

After his examination Du Mu became personal secretary to the governor of Yangzhou, Niu Sengru, with whom he remained for several years. In one of the poems below Du Mu expresses regrets for the life of pleasure that he led during that period in Yangzhou. (This lies on the north side of the lower Yangzi River in Jiangsu Province.) It is said that he knew practically every famous prostitute in this well-known pleasure district and that, unbeknownst to him and on the orders of his good friend Niu Sengru, he was guarded on his visits by thirty soldiers in civilian clothes.

Having returned to Chang'an and Luoyang for a time, Du Mu was then promoted to the post of governor at Huangzhou. The poem 'Early geese' was written there in 842. Several poems refer to the nearby rivers Xiao and Xiang and to the undeveloped wilderness area in Hunan where they meet. Du Mu also served as governor in Chizhou, Muzhou and Huzhou. These all lie south of the Yangzi, in the large area referred to in the translations here both as Jiangnan and as 'South of the River'. In 851 he was admitted to the Imperial Court in Chang'an as a Censor, becoming the secretary in charge of prisons and state secrets. Apart from his poems, Du Mu also wrote a military handbook.

Several of the poems refer to Du Mu's whitening hair and to his (brief) retirement. This he spent at his grandfather's mansion at the 'Red Slope' of page 77. Red Slope was at Fanchuan (Birdcage Brook) near Chang'an. He loved this place where high-ranking officials used to gather and he intended to publish his thousands of poems as the 'Fanchuan Collection'. We have noted already what he actually did with them.

Towards the end of his life Du Mu dreamed that a man told him to change his name to 'Bi', meaning 'finish'. Months later, a servant came to tell him "the meal is almost cooked, but the earthenware has cracked". He took both of these as evil omens and died shortly afterwards, in 852.

THE POEMS AND THEIR TRANSLATION

Most of the poems in this collection consist, in Chinese, of two or four couplets. In each poem the lines are all of either five or seven monosyllables. Amongst the other structural features are the use of rhyme and, in some couplets, of syntactical parallelism: the matching of noun with noun, verb with verb etc. —

> *In bare sand, a tiger's tracks.*
> *On smooth water, dragon spittle.*

As to content, the poetry of the Tang dynasty may seem to abound in non-sequiturs. In part, this is simply because so many poems are occasional and, as in many a painting, there is more to an experience than the point of focus. Often the key lies in cultural or literary allusions that are unfamiliar to the western reader. Thus, for example, many of these poems refer to willows. This is because it was the custom to present willow wands to departing friends, and because many poems were composed on the occasions of such partings.

The first step in translation is understanding. With poems like these this entails some guesswork since they contain few indications of tense and number and usually lack pronouns. If many of the poems are translated in the first person singular, this is more a matter of appropriateness than of textual necessity. Such uncertainties are often largely resolved by ensuring that the poem as a whole makes sense, and not just the individual lines.

Having arrived at a literal translation, my aim has been to express the poem in simple, musical English. I am happiest when the key words in each line correspond to those of the original, with little embroidery. When there is parallelism between the lines of a couplet, I am pleased to retain it, but do not try too hard to accomplish this. In short, I like the poems to remain essentially Du Mu's (though much is inevitably lost) and not to become mine. Often, however, I come to a line that is either hard to put into English, or else simply becomes limp. One possible remedy which avoids the temptation of over-inventiveness is to steal a few words from some better-known English writer. Thus the multitude of Chinese literary allusions may be replaced with a few English ones. There are only five in this collection and nothing is gained by pointing them out.

To be true to Du Mu's poetry, one should rhyme, but this is harder in English than in Chinese and all translators of Tang poetry who consistently use conventional rhyme schemes inevitably distort meaning to some extent. It happens that my own preference — in writing my own poetry for example — is for the irregular use of rhymes and half-rhymes both within lines and and at their ends. This style, for those who like it, seems an ideal compromise for use in translation. Therefore, I explore the available synonyms and list such pairs or groups of rhymes as might be useful. Often, however, there seem to be no rhymes at all worth using. In this way, a consistent approach may lead to formal variety.

With regard to the irregular use of internal rhymes, a curious phenomenon has impressed me. While it is true that some of these may pass unnoticed on casual reading, they do seem sometimes to make one feel the presence of (phantom) rhymes, conventionally at the ends of lines, where actually no rhyme exists at all.

There is another problem of translation that the reader may wish to consider. In the language of these poems there are numerous phrases, usually of two words, that either need not, or else should not, be taken literally, word for word (like English, 'white elephant'). Hopefully, those that should not have not, and are not worth discussion here. More interesting are those that need not, but may, be taken literally, especially those that Du Mu probably intended to be read ambiguously. One such phrase is 'river(s) lake(s)' which may mean simply 'rivers and lakes', but can also indicate that the subject is out of the main stream of affairs (i.e. in the 'backwaters'). Another is 'spring wind' or 'spring breeze', which may refer either to a wind in springtime or else to sexual intercourse. (Of the seasons, Spring and Autumn are mentioned much the most often — in the poetry not only of Du Mu, but of other Tang poets. Often Autumn stands for old age.) In other phrases the words are specific examples of some broader concept for which they stand. Thus 'mountain(s) river(s)' means countryside or kingdom. Likewise 'red blue/green' may stand for a whole painting. In poetry it is sometimes desirable to translate the two words separately, and so retain more colour.

RFB

Plantains
in the Rain

SPENDING THE NIGHT AT YUNZHI TEMPLE: UNABLE TO CROSS THE CURRENT, I TAKE THE RIVERSIDE ROAD

The river spurts between two rocks.
I turn my horse to the broken bridge.
Here, an ancient temple, chilly wind,
cold bells, and rainy sky at dusk.
In bare sand, a tiger's tracks.
On smooth water, dragon spittle.
Back down the river road.
The tide is deep. There is no boat.

行樂及時已晚對酒當歌

歌不成千里暮山重聲

翠一溪簫水淺深清

高人以飲為怡事浮世除詮

盡強名宥著白蘋千欲

吐雪舟相訪勝閒行

湖南王柏松李郎秀才

HUNAN IN EARLY SPRING: AN
INVITATION TO THE SCHOLAR LI YING *

Pleasure must be grasped in time
        and time runs out.
Wine needs song,
        but I cannot sing.
Mountains in the evening,
        a thousand *li* of green on green.
A stream of icy water
        with clear depths, clear shallows.
Men of noble character
        devote themselves to drinking,
but a floating life devoid of verse
        is affectation.
I see some duckweed,
        buds about to burst.
Visits in the snow by boat
        are better than quiet travelling.

ON A SUMMER DAY BY GOU STREAM I SENT OFF
THE SCHOLAR LU PEI.
HE WAS RETURNING TO MOUNT WANGWU,
PLANNING TO TAKE THE CIVIL SERVICE
EXAMINATIONS.

Flags fluttered on the shops in the suburbs.
The first cocoons untwined their silk.
A man waded an azure stream
with his horse tied up to a branch of green poplar.
Slowly, then, his footprints faded.
His heart was abrim with boundless hope.
On autumn hills I mind your parting
and rue that moment of cassia flowers.

IN KAIYUAN TEMPLE IN XUANZHOU: A GIFT TO
THE MONK WEIZHEN.

Once you were a novice on Mount Jing.
The Buddhist way, all know, requires a thousand years.
Night deepens.
        The moon tints this place of Buddha.
The meal ends.
        A bell sounds the time for sutras.
Rain comes through
        — has brought green moss to ancient pictures.
Autumn too
        — and red leaves fall on recent poems.
Do not reject, I beg, this stranger from the river city;
despite the worldly dust and blast,
        I am stirred up with higher hopes.

IN YUE

From Stone City's warmth and flowers,
                    a francolin flew off.
In Spring a wanderer sailed away,
                    in Autumn was not back.
Cherished still as husband,
                    his heart was yet as stone.
Every night, from fine silk,
                    a shuttle wove him winter clothing.

AN AUTUMN VIEW NEAR CHANG'AN

A tower to lean on. Hoary trees about.
A mirror sky with not one wisp.
Southern Mountain, autumn hues:
spirit, power, soaring high.

A GREEN GRAVE *

There's a green grave beside Long's flowing water.
Atop Yan's peak are evening clouds of Autumn.
Here a moth-browed beauty fell to Yellow Springs.
Night after night her lonely spirit grieves beneath the moon.

漓溪春尽碧泱泱，洪洪

水满兰花雨半香，楚国

大去惟悴日应寻此

路去潇湘

兰溪 在蕲州西

ORCHID RIVER *

Orchid River late in Spring, blue, magnificent.
Orchid flowers mirrored in the water, fragrant in the rain.
On that day of suffering the nobleman of Chu
surely sought this road to the rivers Xiao and Xiang.

THOUGHTS OF A TRAVELLER

With windows open, mat and pillow cold,
restless, I think of the Xiao and the Xiang.
When do the colours of the hills grow old?
Men's hearts are busy all day long.
The wind through the pines brings midnight rain.
The moon through the screens falls as frost in the hall.
He's ready to go — is that horse of mine —
back to the rivers where oranges blow.

EARLY GEESE *

By Golden River in mid-autumn
    the enemy draws his bowstring.
Beyond the clouds, in startled flight,
    you part from each other grieving.
The moon shines on Immortal Palms
    as your lone shadows pass
and your sounds reach a dim lamp
    in Long Gate Palace.
You surely know that hordes of Tartar
    riders are about,
so why do you chase the spring wind,
    year after year returning?
Do not disdain the Xiao and Xiang,
    where people are so few;
the waters abound with wild rice,
    the river banks with moss.

OLD HAUNTS

A poem of peonies idly chanted;
pensive longing with eyebrows knitted;
a sideways glance, a distant gaze;
a fine gown and tresses slowly straightened.
Back then to a spring daydream,
smiling, toying with sprays of blossom.
Home is a little Chang Ling market.
Who would know of her existence?

LOVE IN THE WOMEN'S QUARTERS

Loveliness with moon-shaped brows.
Raven tresses newly feigning flight.
Stealthy smoothing of sandalwood powder.
Lined clothes painted in windowed sunlight.
Sleeves red and draping lonesome.
Eyebrows blacked and tightly gathered.
As he leaves for Chang Ling:
"Shall you... Shall you come tonight?"

多情却似總無情唯

覺樽前笑不成蠟燭

有心還惜別替人垂

淚到天明

贈別

26

PARTING I *

Graceful and delicate, just over thirteen,
a cardamom spray, the second month starting.
Ten *li* on the Yangzhou road, with spring winds blowing:
where the beaded curtains lift, it never was the same.

PARTING II

My many loves now seem no love at all.
Behind my cup I only feel a still-born smile.
The candles feel too, and mourn our parting.
For us they drip their tears until the light of dawn.

WRITTEN ON CHANZHI MONASTERY IN YANGZHOU

After rain — one cicada's din;
autumn wind through pine and cinnamon;
green moss on stone steps;
white birds loath to go.
Evening mists enfold the trees,
the sun aslant on little towers.
Who knows the Zhuxi road?
Song and music *are* Yangzhou.

TO JUDGE HAN CHUO AT YANGZHOU *

Mountains misty blue, mysterious, and distant water.
South of the River, as Autumn ends, the grass
                                        has not yet withered.
Above the Bridge of Twenty Four the moon dispels
                                                    the night.
Where is that Adonis giving lessons on his flute?

MOURNING HAN CHUO

We buried him at daybreak at a Shangdu gate.
Coffin cords and pennons followed his spirit.
Back with cold smiles, lamenting our lot,
we called the woman, called the boy,
                    demanding the wine bowl.

CATHARSIS

Dispirited in Jiangnan I wander with wine.
The slim-waisted broke their hearts, light on my palm.
Ten years — then I wakened from my Yangzhou dream,
famed in blue houses as a heartless man.

THE GARDEN AT GOLDEN VALLEY *

The beauty and bustle are but fragrant dust.
The grass of Spring grows tall, unkept,
                and waters flow uncaring.
An east wind brings a bird's sad cry at dusk
as, near the tower where she leaped,
                other flowers now are falling.

ON THE ROAD — A QUATRAIN

Silk hairs in the mirror:
                a sorrow now familiar.
Dust marks on my clothing:
                harder to brush off.
Rueful in backwaters,
                fishing rod in hand.
Yet the western sun is blocked
                as I face Chang'an .

THE SCREEN *

A slender waist, upon a screen that Zhou Fang painted.
Years have passed; the reds and greens have faded.
She leans across the marble sill,
                a girl with phoenix hair.
She strokes the dust, still jealous of such beauty.

BY MA STREAM ON SHANG MOUNTAIN

Sunlit clouds and misty colours gather from
       the four directions.
Willows hang down soft and supple by a dozen
        homes or so.
Pheasants fly and deer pass amid the distant
       fragrant grasses.
There are oxen in the alleys, there are chickens
       in their coops
    as the spring sun slants.

A handsome pair of ancient brows confronts
       a bottle of wine.
His red-sleeved daughters pin flowers in their hair.
I think of the long dusty journey in my carriage
as, ruefully beside the beck, I doodle in fine sand.

REVISITING XIANG AND WEEPING FOR MY DEAD FRIEND, WEI SHOUPENG

My old friend's grave tree stands in the autumn wind.
A void remains — Bo Dao also had no son.
I return to where we parted with music and singing.
Across the river flutes play
            in the bright light of the moon.

雨潛瑞璿階

紫翠虞皇故關河日

到處皆小三峯

趙橫雲八十餘歲小石

WRITTEN ON A SMALL ROCK NEWLY ERECTED IN EIGHT-PINE YARD

Rain falls — shattered pearls.
Mosses grow — rich purple, green.
When shall I reach the ancient watch-tower?
I might as well look at this tiny hill-top!

THE FESTIVAL OF THE NINTH DAY —
CLIMBING HIGH ON MOUNT QI

In Autumn's shadow and river's dank
          the geese begin to fly.
I take my guest and take my jug
          to the mountain's misty green.
It is hard to meet in this world of dust
          and open one's mouth in laughter.
We'll cover our heads with chrysanthemum flowers
          ere we go down again.
But we shall drink our fill of wine
          and toast this festive day.
No need to climb and gaze back down
          to sigh for the setting sun.
From days of old until this time
          it's always been this way.
On Ox Peak (recall the tale!),
          why shed tears alone?

CHIMES *

Several streams of autumn water,
                       and pearl beads hanging.
Fair hands ring
       (ding dong, ding dang!),
                   but fear night's cold.
The music stops,
       yet still she strikes a few notes more.
O dread! that pearly tears should fall
                   on plates of gold!

AN AUTUMN DAY

My plan is this — to work alone in peace
as autumn gusts put an end to ranting.
I'll buy a hill and plant bamboo,
will play my lute in front of guests.
Late smoke will rise from kitchen herbs,
the pestle sounds through pines in the courtyard.
Then shall I find my true self,
ruing my former heart.

CUT BAMBOO

The monastery is abandoned.
                    The bamboos fade.
Officialdom would rather that you stay.
Frosty roots are yielding to the axe.
It's Autumn, and the wind jades tinkle still.
South of the River is a third-rate poet;
is there a place whence sorrows may be banished?

INSOMNIA

Night comes and brings, not dreams,
but thoughts of white about my head.
Few are granted five score years.
Many face ten thousand woes.
O life! thou art a galling load,
a weary path that ends in death.
Speak no word of wealth and fame.
They are my foes — that fame, that wealth!

YOUNG WILLOWS *

Languor,
 stirred by the breeze at daybreak.
Slender waists
 that draw men back to view with envy.
Green
 that does not fully shade the long dyke's water.
Golden catkins
 that greeted Spring's arrival at the park.

All around are breaking hearts that think of far-off roads
— of dusty steps, for which each rain-soaked wand
       is valediction.
Outside the eastern gates the partings are so many
that every morning, every evening, bring more
       grief and sorrow.

A NIGHT IN THE SOUTH TOWER

Flutes of jade, golden goblets,
           through the night unceasing.
The shortness of the day, the flowing years,
           are their obsession.
The sounds of singing softly thread the clear night air
and the moon is lovely by the turquoise tower.

On my pillow — to my surprise — I dream of fishing
and by my lamp feel homesick yet.
I think today of great men's deeds
— I, beside this woman, head already white!

ON THE ROAD TO BINGZHOU

On the road with the army, I weary now,
but who heeds a miserable poet?
It's Spring, but there's snow on the garrison tower.
It's dusk, and the border horn winds through cloud.
I gaze far away, see no-one at all,
with a turn of my head catch a flock of geese leaving.
So how to be rid of that officer,
to doze in a drunken stupor?

SEEING SCHOLAR WU PARTING FROM A COURTESAN

Red candles shorten.
    Qiang flutes moan.
Solo singing ends in sobs.
    Strings from Shu take over.
Ten thousand *li* will part them:
    two lines of tears.
Cold rain shrouds the river,
    deepening despair.

WRITTEN IN ANZHOU, IN THE TOWER OF FLOATING CLOUD TEMPLE, TO OFFICER ZHANG IN HUZHOU

Last summer, after sparse rain,
we leant together on the red rail, chatting.
There was water, then, below the tower;
today, where has it gone?
My sorrows are as many as the blades of grass in Spring
and my thoughts go with the solitary swan.
Why are they so troubled
        — the willows on the river-banks of Chu?
Numberless as catkins are the griefs of parting.

RED CLIFF

A broken spear sunk in sand, the iron not yet rusted:
I take it, rub it clean, and recognize a former dynasty.
Had the east wind not aided General Zhou,
Spring would have locked the two Qiao ladies
                    inside the Bronze Bird Tower.

AN AUTUMN NIGHT

With Autumn's silver candlelight
                        cool on the painted screen,
a little fan of flimsy silk flicks at darting fireflies.
The Plough is cold as water amid the shades of evening.
I lie back and watch the stars
                    — the Weaver-girl and Cowherd.

BEFORE GOING TO WUXING, I CLIMB TO LE'YOU
PLAIN

Peaceful times are to my taste; I have no talent.
In peace, I like the lonesome cloud, the company of monks.
Before I bear my banner to the river and the sea,
I gaze on the tombs of the Emperors, on Le'you plain.

CLIMBING TO LE'YOU PLAIN

In a sea of tranquillity vast and empty a lone bird
                                        fades from view.
Here ten thousand ancient days melt away to nothing.
See what remains of the House of Han
— five tombs, treeless in the autumn wind.

多暇香篆書畫省

庫捕魚兒溪蛇年

鸞飛逸映碧山去一

林翠卷蒼晚風

嬌鶯

EGRETS

With snowy coats, snowy crests, and sapphire bills,
they flock to fish, reflected in the brook.
In startled flight, they shine on emerald hills
— petals from a pear tree in an evening breeze.

THE CUCKOO *

How was Du Yu wronged,
that every year he cries at the Gates of Shu?
Even now he bears a grudge,
forever mourning his lost soul.
The heart is rent by fragrant plants
with red flowers marked with blood.
Spring colours cover the countryside.
To whom may he tell his grief?

RHODODENDRONS

On little hills the rhododendrons blaze like fire
— beauty disdainful amid much beauty.
A single flower on a lady's jade hairpin
seems to flame in her dark cloud-hair.

A TOWER BY THE YANGZI RIVER

Alone, I pour out spring wine,
then climb the tower half tipsy.
Who startled the line of geese
that broke through the Yangzi clouds?

THE PARROT *

An ornate hall. The sun is slowly rising.
A carved perch, and leash of red ribbon.
Home was once the mountain trees of Long,
but the beautiful lady has golden scissors.

Avoiding his cage, he tucks his green tail
and, with beak ajar, looks for new feathers.
Far from his mind is the third gold monkey's silence.
Such is the way of the world!

WRITTEN IN THE WATER PAVILION OF KAIYUAN
TEMPLE IN XUANZHOU *

Where the Six Dynasties flourished, grass meets sky.
Where clouds laze in a tranquil heaven,

past meets present.
Birds go, birds come, amongst the colours of the hills.
Men sing, men cry. amid the sounds of water.
A curtain in deep Autumn is rain on a thousand homes.
A flute heard at sunset is wind about the tower.
Sad am I that I cannot meet Fan Li.
Ragged misty forest lies eastward from Five Lakes.

ALLEGORY

Warm breeze, spring days,
    a willow newly blown,
reflecting on his 'is' and 'was',
    with shame.
Alone, why should he rue the morrow?
There's blossoming apricot South of the River.

鉴赏苦此修，惟意所有为

懒意所有月为雪里

阳阳易易

毛泽

BASIN POND

Picks broke the green-mossed clod.
It stole a slip of sky.
White clouds spawn in the depths of the mirror.
The bright moon dips at the step.

A VISIT TO XU YAN *

A door near the cool stream.
   Windows to the hills.
Pillowed on a knoll
   by the ever-burbling flow.
Long looking down on the shady of this world
that always deal in dirt,
   with no yen for laughter.

CLOUDS

East and west without restraint:
where you came from who can tell?
This morning over vast Dongting;
this evening back to deep Wu gorge.
You cross the river with the shadows of birds
and hug the trees where gibbons call.
Do not go to hide in Gaotang;
dry shoots wait for your downpour.

GRAFFITI ON A TOWER IN QI'AN CITY

A sob grates on the river tower,
    a blast from a horn.
Across the cold shore falls a flood of pale sunlight.
It's pointless to lean at the balustrade,
    looking back sadly.
Home is seventy five rest-huts away.

IN QI'AN, AN OCCASIONAL POEM

Above the bridge that spans the stream,
    the setting sun is two poles high.
There's a light mist of cut floss
    in the shadow of the willows.
How many green lotus stems
    lean on each other sorrowing?
All at once they turn their heads,
    with the west wind behind them.

HOU POND, IN QI'AN

Water chestnuts pierce the floating duckweed
    in a pool of green brocade.
Summer orioles twitter in their thousands
    playing amongst roses.
All day long there's not a soul
    to watch the drizzle with me.
Side by side, a duck and drake
    bathe in scarlet coats.

BIAN RIVER BLOCKED BY ICE

One thousand *li*; the river's length begins to freeze
and horse jades and fine jade pendants
    sound their fitful cadence.
The drift of life is just like this
    — like water under ice,
flowing eastward day and night,
    unknown.

IDLE LINES

Where the man is, there is home:
a hundred *yi* of gold, a single bloom.
Tell me where spring winds blow sweet.
Green poplars, deep lanes, horse's head atilt!

THE GIBBON

White moon, grey mist,
    and dark flowing water.
A lone gibbon with a grudge
    cries out in mid-Autumn
— three sounds almost sundered,
    as if his heart would sunder too.
Though he is of tender age,
    yet his head is touched with white.

IN SYMPATHY FOR A GIBBON

He plucks a plum blossom alone in South Garden
and searches all the secret mossy holes.
Then he's startled in the tree tops
               by a chance gust of evening,
seems to falter on his long branch,
               and wants to come down.

THE LONE WILLOW

A single willow, full of mist,
sweeps the earth, sways always in the wind.
Fair lady cannot bear to pluck from it;
wistfully she stays her slender hand.

IN A HUFF

Calm is the way, and calm the turning seasons.
The time has come, but not the call.
Reason, surely, to leave this town
and live at ease in Mount Bo's combe.

MEETING AN OLD FRIEND

For years not having met,
we meet, and yet with sadness
and with tears like sleet.
(Your hair, alas, resembles silk.)
In grief, each grips the other's hand.
It is the time of falling flowers, too.
Do not begrudge our tipsiness tonight;
brief life is here our portion.

THE GRAVES OF THE PALACE WOMEN

All have left the palace, those ladies of the court.
A garden wall outside the city — there a string of graves.
They entered young, were taught to sing and dance,
never knew their king, ere each grew old.

A PALACE TALE

Silk light as cicada wings,
   red around her body.
Jade skin and tipsy air,
   a spring breeze rising.
Shut deep in the palace,
   in doubt and hesitation,
she tries more red powder
   at the Emperor's call.

Palace eunuchs lead her out.
   The doors briefly open.
As decreed, she's led to court,
   but finds no favour.
Still, they take the silver key;
   the golden lock is fastened.
The moon is bright.
Petals fall
   in yet another dusk.

ON THE NANLING ROAD

Nanling's waters — vast, so vast.
Strong winds, light clouds, heralding Autumn.
Just here the traveller's lonely heart turns back.
Whose red sleeves are those,
   leaning on the river tower?

A SONG OF STOCKINGS

Measured by filigree footrule:
    four lines shorter.
Delicate jade bamboo-shoot fingers
    bind her light clouds.
A youth of Five Tombs bamboozles her, tipsy.
In front of that flower he smiles
    as they peep from its painted skirts.

A MOUNTAIN WALK

Far up Cold Mountain slants a rocky path.
There, where clouds are born, are people's dwellings.
Halt the carriage. Sit. Enjoy the maple woods at dusk.
The frosted leaves are redder far
                    than flowers that bloom in March.

AN OLD MONK SENT BACK TO THE SECULAR WORLD *

With snowy hair, not yet one inch,
in Autumn's cold and grown quite weak,
he seeks, alone, a path amongst the leaves
and carries still a remnant of his robe.
The sun, his sun, is all but set.
About him are a thousand peaks.
Where shall he go?
To that he knows no answer.

LAMENT FOR A FLOWER

This I regret —
    that, seeking fragrance, I arrive too late.
Seen already years ago, the time to open not yet come;
now this wind-swayed tattered bloom,
green leaves' shade and branches full of fruit.

A MAT OF VARIEGATED BAMBOO *

Blood-stained streaks, that form a striped brocade,
a hundred years of anguish, here to this day.
Well we know that these are Xiang wives' tears.
How can we bear to sleep upon their traces?

千里鶯啼綠映紅

水村山郭酒旗風

朝四百八十寺多少

樓臺烟雨中 江南春絕句

SPRING SOUTH OF THE RIVER

Orioles sang in a thousand hamlets,
    red glowing on green.
Waterside villages, mountain ramparts,
    wineshop pennants blowing.
Of four hundred and eighty temples,
    those of the Southern Dynasties,
how many towers are there now
    in misty rain?

THE CRANE *

A clear sound, to greet the evening moon.
Sad thoughts, standing in cold rushes.
A red crown, and Xi Shi cheeks.
Hoary feathers in a 'Four Hao' beard.

The blue clouds have restless ways
and white egrets manners rather vulgar.
So, all the day, he has no group of friends,
But, lonely by the stream, consoles his shadow.

TO A HUNTSMAN ON HORSEBACK

Two eagles have fallen already,
          and the blood is still fresh.
Whips crack and horses run.
          Bodies plunge again.
I trust, Sir, that you'll not shoot
          a wild goose from the South
for fear it bear a letter
          sent from far away.

ROAMING THE BORDER

Yellow sands right to the sea;
     on the road there is no dust.
The grass at the border is a long time dry
     with not a sign of Spring.
I pass the foot of Fuyun Mound
     just as the sun is setting.
Then, with my horse, I chance to meet
     an archer hunting eagles.

FISHERMAN

White-haired in Canglang
quite without care.
Line down in autumn deeps,
Boat back with the night moon.
Mist and shadow steal across the reed bank,
the tide-mark at his bamboo door.
All year round with gulls for friends,
coming, going, free of guile.

THE SOUTH TOWER OF KAIYUAN
MONASTERY IN XUANZHOU

A tiny turret, with space for one bunk crosswise.
All day a view of mountains, flowing wine.
A gentle breeze brings rain at night. Alas,
too drunk! The patter on the window is in vain.

DRINKING ALONE

Through the window, wind and snow.
I hug the stove, with wine crock open.
How about fishing from a boat in the rain,
with an awning for sleep on the autumn flow?

TO SOMEONE FAR AWAY

All the day I beg the man to tell my fortune
and every time he gives good news.
A while ago you went away,
but enter now my dreams.

TEA MOUNTAIN ON A SPRING DAY, TOO ILL TO
DRINK WINE
(presented to a guest)

Music and song aboard the boat.
                              (How picturesque it was!
There were ten days to go before the Sweeping
                              of the Tombs.)
Dainty mountain, smooth white clouds,
light on the stream, like a fresh red bloom,
buds eager, but not quite bursting,
sky half sunny, half in darkness.
Who'd have guessed this ailing judge
could still make 'Tea Immortal'.

A TRAVELLER'S NIGHT

At an inn, without his friends,
the traveller broods despondent and
in lantern's chill remembers.
Comes fitful slumber — till a stray goose ends it —
then dreams, near dawn, of distant home
whence letters come a year delayed.
Yet lovely is the misty moon on Xiang's flow.
Beside the door is moored an angler's boat.

芭蕉为雨移坶阳窗荫

娇怜渠眼滴声尚泙

归乡萝梦遠莫归乡

觉来一蓼蓼　芭蕉

68

PLANTAINS

For the way that plantains move in the rain
I grew some facing the window.
I'm at one with the ditch, for the sound of the dripping
carries me back in a dream to my homeland.
A vain dream: I'll never go home.
I wake from my sleep, turn over again.

RAIN

Cloud upon cloud as far as the frontier, building up
                                    in the distance.
Drips on the curtains, and onto the lanterns,
                                    add to the desolation.
A sleepless night for a lonely guest:
the host has plantains outside the windows.

ON PASSING THE PALACE OF FLORAL PURITY
(a quatrain) *

Returning to Chang'an, I gaze at the heaped
                                        embroidery
of the mountain peak. A thousand doorways open
                                        one by one.
There's a rider with his red dust, and a smiling
                                        royal concubine,
but no-one really knows if it is the lichees coming.

MOORING ON THE QINHUAI *

With mist on cold water, moon on sand,
we moor at night on the Qinhuai,
tying up close to a tavern.
The merchants' daughters do not know
the pain of a kingdom overrun,
and yet they sing, across the river,
the Harem Flower Song.

THE DEPARTURE OF A CRANE

He flies alone, while others flock.
Shafts of six feathers press on the wind.
His sound is lost beyond blue clouds.
A single silhouette crosses the moon.
It's a long way back above green fields
to the empty nest on a red-barked cinnamon.
Does he know where his strong wings take him?
There is no end to the sky.

SETTING OUT EARLY

I hang my whip and give the horse his head.
For several *li* we hear no cockcrow.
Into the woods, my dreams still linger
and I start from time to time at flying leaves.
It's frosty, and a lone crane wheels.
The moon still tarries above the distant hills.
My servant speaks no further word of danger;
it is a peaceful time, a peaceful road again.

SPRING THOUGHTS

Why is time in such a hurry?
All of a sudden it's Spring again.
Who governs the bright moon?
The country's rulers change unseen.
Blossoms, orioles age unnoticed.
Joys and glories turn to dust.
I think of willows by a far red door:
partings must become more frequent.

IN SORROW FOR A FRIEND WHO MOURNS A FLUTE-PLAYING COURTESAN *

The jade flute's sound is stopped
            and lost in the flowing years.
Eyes fill with spring sorrow
            and the grave tree is misty.
Already had her beauty followed
            the scattered clouds and rain.
The phoenix tower is empty, locked.
            The moon is still as bright.

THE HAN RIVER

Mighty waters rolling ever. White gulls flying.
Green and pure, spring-deep, good to dye clothing in.
Going northward. Coming southward.
                              Man's inevitable ageing.
Setting sun. Protracted parting. Fishing boats
                                          returning.

LOOKING FOR A READING COMPANION

Once, I remember, not knowing the Way,
I'd envy the fish, when down by the river.
Now that I've travelled and seen the world,
I'm far too ill for endeavour.
In Autumn's drizzle I plant bamboo
and I read at night by a single lantern.
I'm hoping you'd like to do so too
and spend your old age by the mountain.

MINDING THE SPRING

Spring is half over. The year is turning.
Little more remains.
And so we toast the fading flowers
and taste December wine together.
Sad cups bid the Spring farewell.
Humble besoms sweep up petals.
Who can stop the eastward flow?
Year by year old age comes closer.

A CLEAR STREAM IN CHIZHOU

I play in the stream all day until dusk.
Numbered with my autumns are my whitening hairs.
What have you washed a thousand times over?
My brush-head soon will bear no trace of dust.

LAMENT FOR SPRING

Flowers open. Flowers fall.
The seasons move in secret ways.
No trick prolongs the days of Spring.
How can those of youth be stayed?
Low shrubs newly strewn with butterflies,
tall willows where cicadas sing:
where does all the beauty go?
Cuckoos call amongst the hills.

HOMECOMING *

Children tug his clothes and ask:
why so long in coming home?
with whom compete in years and months
to win those silk-white sideburns?

煙深苔苍唱樵兒苍落寞輕儂

客歸藤岸竹洲相掩映滿池春

雨鸝鵜飛乳肥春洞生鵝管沼

避迴巖勢大开目笑卷懷頭、

角縮歸鹽烟磴哈如哨

朱地絶句

RED SLOPE
(second quatrain of three)

Mossy lanes in deep mist, woodcutters singing,
falling flowers, a light chill, weary wanderer's return.
Bank of vines and bamboo islet shade each other's image.
Ponds are full with spring rain. Dabchicks are flying.

RED SLOPE
(third quatrain of three) *

Plump breasts of stalactite; spring grottos sprouting
                                        goose quills.
Jaggy crags make dog's teeth with the zigzag of the pool.
I laugh at myself, 'curled in the bosom' and with
                                        horns pulled in,
then wind back up the misty steps, just like a snail.

Chinese Texts
with Notes and Finding List

Chinese texts for the poems translated in this book are reproduced on the following pages, with the exception of those poems which are accompanied by Joseph Lo's original calligraphy.

Below the Chinese texts, there is a reference to the page number of every poem in one of the recent editions of Du Mu's poetry, *Fanchuan shiji zhu*, Feng Jiwu zhu, Beijing: Zhonghua shuju, 1962. Where there is a note by the translator, this is also given, beside the page reference.

Please note: this is a basic text, to be used only as a first point of reference. For textual variants and so forth, please compare the existing Chinese editions.

嗟投雲智寺，渡溪不得，却取沿江路往

雙巖瀉一川，回馬斷橋前，古廟陰風地，寒鐘暮雨天；沙虛留虎跡，水滑帶龍涎。却下臨江路，潮深無渡船。

句溪夏日送盧霈秀才歸王屋山將欲赴舉

野店正紛泊，繭蠶初引絲。 行人碧溪渡，繫馬綠楊枝。 苒苒跡始去，悠悠心所期。 秋山念君別，惆悵桂花時。

宣州開元寺贈惟真上人

曾與徑山爲小師，千年僧行眾人知：夜深月色當禪處，齋後鐘聲到講時。 經雨綠苔侵古畫，過秋紅葉落新詩。 勸君莫厭江城客！雖在風塵別有期。

越中

石城花暖鷓鴣飛，征客春帆秋不歸。 猶自保郎心似石，綾梭夜夜織寒衣。

長安秋望

樓倚霜樹外，鏡天無一毫。 南山與秋色，氣勢兩相高。

青塚

青塚前頭隴水流，燕山山上暮雲秋。蛾眉一墜窮泉路，夜夜孤魂月下愁。

旅情

窗虛枕簟涼，寢倦憶瀟湘，山色幾時老，人心終日忙。松風半夜雨，簾
月滿堂霜。匹馬好歸去，江頭橘正香。

早鴈

金河秋半虜弦開，雲外驚飛四散哀。仙掌月明孤影過，長門燈暗數聲來。須知胡騎紛
紛在，豈逐春風一一迴？莫厭瀟湘少人處，水多菰米岸莓苔。

舊遊

閑吟芍藥詩，悵望久顰眉。盼盼迴眸遠，纖衫整髻遲。重尋春晝夢，笑把淺花枝。小
市長陵住，非郎誰得知？

閨情

娟娟卻月眉，新鬢學鴉飛。暗砌勻檀粉，晴窗畫夾衣。袖紅垂寂寞，眉黛斂依稀。還
向長陵去，今宵歸不歸？

Pages 21–25

332 Yellow Springs = Hades.

219 Here Du Mu, feeling that his talents were not being put to proper use, identifies himself with Qu Yuan, an incorruptible and ill-fated scholar who suffered a similar disappointment. The orchid is associated with Qu Yuan and symbolizes his purity.

341

237 The Immortal Palms and Long Gate Palace were both in the capital, Chang'an. In this poem Du Mu expresses his anxiety about an imminent invasion from the north. The geese may represent the endangered people of the border region.

300

300

贈別

娉娉嫋嫋十三餘，荳蔻梢頭二月初。春風十里揚州路，卷上珠簾總不如。

題揚州禪智寺

雨過一蟬噪，飄蕭松桂秋。青苔滿階砌，白鳥故遲留。暮靄生深樹，斜陽下小樓。誰知竹西路，歌吹是揚州。

寄揚州韓綽判官

青山隱隱水遙遙，秋盡江南草木凋。二十四橋明月夜，玉人何處敎吹簫？

哭韓綽

平明送葬上都門，紼翣交橫逐去魂。歸來冷笑悲身事，喚婦呼兒索酒盆。

遣懷

落魄江南載酒行，楚腰腸斷掌中輕。十年一覺揚州夢，占得青樓薄倖名。

金谷園

繁華事散逐香塵，流水無情草自春。日暮東風怨啼鳥，落花猶似墮樓人。

Pages 27–30

311 Because of the form of its pistils, the cardamom is a symbol of love.

311

198

282 On the Bridge of Twenty Four in Yangzhou in former times two dozen beautiful ladies used to play their flutes.

250

369

337 This garden near Luoyang belonged to Shi Chong (249–300 AD), a very rich man, cruel and extravagant, whose favourite concubine, Lu Zhu (Green Pearl), was coveted by a certain general. Unable to obtain her by fair means, the latter falsified an imperial decree for the arrest of Shi Chong. While soldiers were siezing him, Lu Zhu shut herself in a high room and

途中一絕

鏡中絲髮悲來慣，衣上塵痕拂漸難。　惆悵江湖釣竿手，却遮西日向長安。

屏風絕句

屏風周防畫纖腰，歲久丹青色半銷。　斜倚玉窗鬟髮女，拂塵猶自妬嬌饒。

商山麻澗

雲光嵐彩四面合，柔柔垂柳十餘家。　雉飛鹿過芳草遠，牛巷雞塒春日斜。　秀眉老父對樽酒，蒨袖女兒簪野花〔二〕。　征車自念塵土計，惆悵溪邊書細沙。

重到襄陽哭亡友韋壽朋

故人墳樹立秋風，伯道無兒跡更空。　重到笙歌分散地，隔江吹笛月明中。

九日齊山登高

江涵秋影鴈初飛，與客攜壺上翠微。　塵世難逢開口笑，菊花須插滿頭歸。　但將酩酊酬佳節，不用登臨恨落暉。　古往今來只如此，牛山何必獨霑衣。

方響

數條秋水挂琅玕，玉手丁當怕夜寒。　曲盡連敲三四下，恐驚珠淚落金盤。

Pages 31–37

jumped to her death from the window. 'Fragrant dust' could be taken to mean 'sweet memories', but it is a Buddhist phrase referring to the six 'dusts' that may soil a pure mind, namely smell, colour, sound, taste, touch and ideas.

298

250 Zhou Fang was an outstanding painter of portraits and erotic pictures. Some of the portraits are now in the Palace Museum of Taiwan.

263

270

252

209

372 'Autumn water' can mean 'limpid eyes'. Thus the first line could read 'Several streams from limpid eyes...'

秋日

有計自安業，秋風罷遠吟，買山惟種竹，對客更彈琴。　煙起藥廚晚，杵聲松院深。　閒眠得眞性，惆悵舊時心。

斫竹

寺廢竹色死，官家寧爾留。　霜根漸隨斧，風玉伨敲秋。　江南苦吟客，何處送悠悠。

不寐

到晚不成夢，思量塡白頭，多無百年命，長有萬般愁！　世路應難盡，營生卒未休，莫言名與利，名利是身讎。

新柳

無力搖風曉色新，細腰爭姤看來頻。　綠蔭未覆長堤水，金穗先迎上苑春。　幾處傷心懷遠路，一枝和雨送行塵。　東門門外多離別，愁殺朝朝暮暮人。

南樓夜

玉管金罇夜不休，如悲晝短惜年流。　歌聲褭褭徹清夜，月色娟娟當翠樓。　枕上暗驚垂釣夢，燈前偏起別家愁。　思量今日英雄事，身到簪裾已白頭。

Pages 38–41

并州道中

行役我方倦，苦吟誰復聞。　戍樓春帶雪，邊角暮吹雲。　極目無人迹，迴頭送鴈羣。　如
何遣公子，高臥醉醺醺。

見吳秀才與池妓別因成絕句

紅燭短時羌笛怨，清歌咽處蜀絃高。　萬里分飛兩行淚，滿江寒雨正蕭騷。

題安州浮雲寺樓寄湖州張郎中

去夏疎雨餘，同倚朱欄語。當時樓下水，今日到何處？恨如春草多，
事與孤鴻去。　楚岸柳何窮，別愁紛若絮。

赤壁

折戟沉沙鐵未銷，自將磨洗認前朝。　東風不與周郎便，銅雀春深鎖二喬。

秋夕

紅燭秋光冷畫屏，輕羅小扇撲流螢。　瑤階夜色涼如水，坐看牽牛織女星。

Pages 42–44

334

248

86–87

271 Red Cliff is on the Yangzi River. Here the fleet of the king of
Wei was destroyed in 208 AD by two generals when it came
down river to attack the kingdoms of Shu and Wu. Had the
king of Wei been more successful, he would have taken the
two famous beauties to his palace, but with the aid of the east
wind General Zhou won a decisive victory with his fire ships.

377

将赴吳興登樂遊原一絕

清時有味是無能，閒愛孤雲靜愛僧。 欲把一麾江海去，樂遊原上望昭陵。

登樂遊原

長空澹澹孤鳥沒，萬古銷沉向此中。 看取漢家何似業，五陵無樹起秋風。

杜鵑

杜宇竟何冤，年年叫蜀門？ 至今銜積恨，終古弔殘魂。 芳草迷腸結[二]，紅花染血痕。

山川盡春色，鳴咽復誰論？

山石榴

似火山榴映小山，繁中能薄艷中閒。 一朵佳人玉釵上，秖疑燒却翠雲鬟。

江樓

獨酌芳春酒，登樓已半醺。 誰驚一行鴈，衝斷過江雲。

鸚鵡

華堂日漸高，雕檻繫紅絛。 故國隴山樹，美人金剪刀。 避籠交翠尾，罅嘴靜新毛。 不

念三緘事，世途皆爾曹。

Pages 45–50

185

140

241

340 An exiled prince of Shu (Sichuan) was turned into a cuckoo so
that he might return each year. It was customary to call at the
Gates of Shu for justice. The red flowers marked with blood
are 'cuckoo flowers', one of the azaleas or rhododendrons
(both of which came to Europe from Sichuan).

235

340

239 'The third gold monkey's silence': the original phrase makes
no literal sense but refers to a story about Confucius. Seeing
three golden statues in a temple, he sealed their lips and

題宣州開元寺水閣閣下宛溪夾溪居人

六朝文物草連空，天澹雲閒今古同。鳥去鳥來山色裏，人歌人哭水聲中。　深秋簾幕千家雨，落日樓臺一笛風。　悵恨無因見范蠡，參差烟樹五湖東。

寓言

暖風遲日柳初含，顧影看身又自慚。　何事明朝獨悵恨，杏花時節在江南。

訪許顏

門近寒溪窗近山，枕山流水日潺潺。　長嫌世上浮雲客，老向塵中不解顏。

雲

東西那有礙，出處豈虛心。　曉入洞庭闊，暮歸巫峽深。　渡江隨鳥影，擁樹隔猿吟。　莫隨高唐去，枯苗待作霖。

題齊安城樓

鳴軋江樓角一聲，微陽瀲瀲落寒汀。　不用憑欄苦迴首，故鄉七十五長亭。

Pages 50–55

wrote an inscription on their backs saying, 'These men choose their words carefully.' Better known in the West is the monkey that speaks no evil.

202 Fan Li was a statesman of the Spring and Autumn Period (722–484 BC).

330

318

331 There is a pun on Xu Yan's name in the last line of the original. Something like it reappears if the Wade spelling 'Yen' is used, but the English word 'yen' is from the Chinese 'yin'.

336

212

齊安郡中偶題

兩竿落日溪橋上，半縷輕煙柳影中。　多少綠荷相倚恨，一時迴首背西風。

齊安郡後池絕句

菱透浮萍綠錦池，夏鶯千囀弄薔薇。　盡日無人看微雨，鴛鴦相對浴紅衣。

汴河阻凍

千里長河初凍時，玉珂瑤珮響參差。　浮生恰似冰底水，日夜東流人不知。

閑題

男兒所在即爲家，百鎰黃金一朵花。　借問春風何處好？綠楊深巷馬頭斜。

猿

月白煙青水暗流，孤猿銜恨叫中秋。　三聲欲斷疑腸斷，饒是少年須白頭。

傷猿

獨折南園一朵梅，重尋幽坎已生苔。　無端晚吹驚高樹，似裊長枝欲下來。

獨柳

含煙一株柳，拂地搖風久。　佳人不忍折，悵望迴纖手。

遣懷

道泰時還泰，時來命不來。　何當離城市，高臥博山隈。

逢故人

年年不相見，相見却成悲。　教我淚如霰，嗟君髮似絲。　正傷攜手處，況值落花時。　莫惜今宵醉，人間忽忽期。

宮人塚

盡是離宮院中女，苑牆城外塚纍纍。　少年入內教歌舞，不識君王到老時。

宮詞二首

蟬翼輕綃傅體紅，玉膚如醉向春風。　深宮鎖閉猶疑惑，更取丹沙試辟宮。

監宮引出暫開門，隨例須朝不是恩。　銀鑰却收金鎖合，月明花落又黃昏。

南陵道中

南陵水面漫悠悠，風緊雲輕欲變秋。　正是客心孤迥處，誰家紅袖憑江樓。

詠襪

鈿尺裁量減四分，纖纖玉筍裹輕雲。　五陵年少欺他醉，笑把花前出畫裙。

山行

遠上寒山石徑斜，白雲生處有人家。　停車坐愛楓林晚，霜葉紅於二月花。

還俗老僧

雪髮不長寸，秋寒力更微。　獨尋一徑葉，猶挈衲殘衣﹝五﹞。　日莫千峯裏，不知何處歸。

歎花

自恨尋芳到已遲，往年曾見未開時。　如今風擺花狼藉，綠葉成陰子滿枝。

Pages 59–61

363

365

322

242 This is just one monk of a quarter million who were turned out when the Emperor closed down 4,600 monasteries in about 846 AD.

369

斑竹筒簟

血染斑斑成錦紋，昔年遺恨至今存。 分明知是湘妃泣，何忍將身臥淚痕。

鶴

清音迎晚月，愁思立寒蒲。 丹頂西施頰，霜毛四皓鬚。 碧雲行止躁，白鷺性靈粗。 日無羣伴，溪邊弔影孤。 終

贈獵騎

已落雙鵰血尚新，鳴鞭走馬又翻身。 憑君莫射南來鴈，恐有家書寄遠人。

遊邊

黃沙連海路無塵，邊草長枯不見春。 日暮拂雲堆下過，馬前逢著射鵰人。

漁父

白髮滄浪上，全忘是與非。 秋潭垂釣去，夜月叩船歸。 煙影侵蘆岸，潮痕在竹扉。 年狎鷗鳥，來去且無機。 終

Pages 61–65

352 When the two wives of Shun cried at his tomb near Lake Dongting, their tears of blood stained the bamboo there. One wife threw herself into the River Xiang and became its water goddess.

201

239 Xi Shi was a famous beauty of the Spring and Autumn Period. The 'Four Hao' were white-haired recluses.

376

338

334

宣州開元寺南樓

小樓纔受一床橫，終日看山酒滿傾。可惜和風夜來雨，醉中虛度打窗聲。

獨酌

窗外正風雪，擁爐開酒缸。何如釣船雨，篷底睡秋江。

寄遠人

終日求人卜，迴迴道好音。那時離別後，入夢到如今。

春日茶山病不飲酒因呈賓客

笙歌登畫船，十日清明前。山秀白雲膩，溪光紅粉鮮。欲開未開花，半陰半晴天。誰

知病太守，猶得作茶仙。

旅宿

旅館無良伴，凝情自悄然。寒燈思舊事，斷鴈警愁眠。遠夢歸侵曉，家書到隔年。湘

江好煙月，門繫釣魚船。

雨

連雲接塞添迢遞，灑幕侵燈送寂寥。一夜不眠孤客耳，主人窗外有芭蕉。

過華清宮絕句

長安廻望繡成堆，山頂千門次第開。一騎紅塵妃子笑，無人知是荔枝來。

泊秦淮

煙籠寒水月籠沙，夜泊秦淮近酒家。商女不知亡國恨，隔江猶唱後庭花。

別鵠

分飛共所從，六翮勢催風。聲斷碧雲外，影孤明月中。青田歸遠路，丹桂舊巢空。矯

早行

冥知何處？天涯不可窮。

僕休辭險〔五〕，時平路復平。

垂鞭信馬行，數里未雞鳴。林下帶殘夢，葉飛時忽驚。霜凝孤鶴迥，月曉遠山橫。僮

Pages 69–71

388

364

138 Lichees were carried to the palace by horsemen riding day
and night for a week from the south. Such extravagance,
which Du Mu deplored, not only wasted the taxpayer's
money, but cost the lives of many men and horses. 'Red dust'
is not only a figure for the life of pleasure and worldly dis-
tractions, but was also applied to the lichee.

273 The Qinhuai, south of the Yangzi from Yangzhou, flows
through Nanjing. It too was a centre for merry-making.

342

343

春懷

年光何太急，倏忽又青春。明月誰家主，江山暗換人。鶯花潛遞老，榮樂漸成塵。遙憶朱門柳，別離應更頻。

傷友人悼吹簫妓

玉簫聲斷沒流年，滿目春愁隴樹煙。艷質已隨雲雨散，鳳樓空鎖月明天。

漢江

溶溶漾漾白鷗飛，綠淨春深好染衣。南去北來人自老，夕陽長送釣船歸。

卜居招書侶

憶昔 一作意壯 未知道，臨川每羨魚，世途行處見，人事病來疎。 微雨秋栽竹，孤燈夜讀書。憐君亦同志，晚歲傍山居。

惜春

春半年已除，其餘強爲有。即此醉殘花，便同嘗臘酒。悵望送春杯，殷勤掃花帚。誰爲駐東流，年年長在手。

池州清溪

弄溪終日到黃昏，照數秋來白髮根。 何物賴君千遍洗？ 筆頭塵土漸無痕。

惜春

花開又花落，時節暗中遷。 無計延春日，何能駐一作留少年。 小叢初散蝶，高柳卽聞蟬。 繁艷歸何處？ 滿山啼杜鵑。

歸家

稚子牽衣問，歸來何太遲？ 共誰爭歲月，贏得鬢邊絲。

Pages 74–77

215

412

364 This poem has also been attributed to Zhao Gu.

169

169 Du Mu returned to Red Slope, near his childhood home, shortly before his death. The last two lines refer to his retirement from office.

Another Recent Wellsweep Publication

Poems of the West Lake
translations from the Chinese

by A. C. Graham

Professor Graham, translator of the Penguin Classics *Poems of the Late T'ang*, visited the famous Chinese beauty spot near Hangzhou in 1984. This book of thirty-odd poems, dating from the 8th to the 16th century, was the result. Each translation is accompanied by the original text in calligraphy by Joseph Lo.

£4.95 (both editions)

64 pp., 20 ill., 210x130, paper, June 1990
trade edition (laminated cover)   0 948454 07 5
reader's edition (laid paper cover)   0 948454 57 1

Order direct (adding 10% to cover postage) and write to be put on the Wellsweep mailing list:

Wellsweep Press
719 Fulham Road
London SW6 5UL
Fax: (+44 71) 731 8009